chad morgan
& other poems

chad morgan

meekling press 2022

Meekling Press
Chicago, IL
meeklingpress.com

Printed in the USA.

Cover photograph by Cameron Crum Crumley

ISBN 978-1-950987-24-5

Library of Congress Control Number: 2022939086

for bob, who was on my lap or nearby throughout the writing of each of these poems & whose paw prints are all over everything.

contents

Who shared a room with his brother until the third grade. Who liked to watch *Meet Me in St. Louis* and listen to Janet Jackson on Cassette. Who was afraid of the dark & Sylvester Stallone in *Judge Dredd*. Who hated to get his clothes dirty at recess. Who went to private school. Who was friends with mostly girls. Who put on plays with his sisters in the basement. Who paused the soundtrack to *Pocahontas* to act out the scenes between songs. Who hated to be John Smith, or even Kocoum. Who has a Black father and a white mother. Who Mr. Wycoff said was "very charismatic." Who was obsessed with Michelle Pfeiffer in *Batman Returns*. Who would fast-forward through the scenes she wasn't in. Who did this over and over until finally he was gay. Who used to pout if he couldn't sit next to his mother at the movies. Who was so bad at math he needed a tutor that summer. Who failed Algebra II. Who had a crush on all of his brother's friends, even Kyle Leeper. Who smoked cigarettes with Alayna & listened to "Cecilia" by Simon & Garfunkel. Who listened to *Daydream* over & over. Who got fired from that restaurant. & that one. & that one too. Who was stoned for most of that year. Who that semester did very poorly in every class except Introduction to Critical Theory. Who watches too much television. Who doesn't drink enough water. Who was always late to first hour. Who learned the choreography to "Lady Marmalade" & performed it at Kevin Cox's birthday party that year, scandalizing the parents, embarrassing everyone. Who is not without a questionable sexual history. Who has a B.A. in English. Who took too long to get it. Who came out to Kara Bowers in the eighth grade. Who tried not to be. Who prayed for forgiveness. Who sang in the madrigal choir and the church choir. Who was best friends with James until he wasn't. Who stood with the Pacific tiding around him off the coast of Mexico. Who bickered with his sister the entire time. Who got swimmer's ear from the water and had to fly back that way. Who can quote at length from *The Golden Girls*. Who has a M.F.A. in Poetry. Who keeps an exhaustive list of everyone who offends him. Who sets aside a certain amount of time each month to plotting revenge. Who wastes a lot of time. Who has lost some things. Who is recovering them, slowly. Lover of Beth & of Mandy. Lover of Nick & of Janae. Lover of Paul & of Dana. Lover of Roz & of James. Lover of Sue. Lover of Alyssa & Eric. Lover of Gregor & Ashley. Lover of Greg. Lover of Tammy. Lover of Lori. Lover of Ron. Lover of Kinsley & Hunter. Lover of Adam. Lover of Courtney. Lover of Grandpa Joe. Lover of Carol. Lover of Jeanette. Lover of John. Lover of Dad. Lover of Mom. Lover of Matt. Lover of Amanda. Lover of Brittany. Lover of Sean. Lover of Josh. Lover of Payton. Lover of Adaira. Lover of Elias. Lover of Royce. Lover of Caleb. Lover of Callie. Lover of Zeke. Lover of Zekiah. Lover of Auggie. Lover of Seely. Lover of Archer. Lover of Shiloh. Lover of Bob.

·

Who Could Ask for Anything More?

I want to feel improbable & sit in a chair incorrectly.
I'm an American so I have to believe I'm exceptional.
I meet a man for drinks & he's perfect except his eyes
are too close together so of course I focus on that.
I drink my martinis very quickly & I tell him *You are perfect*
except your eyes are too close together. I'm not even that drunk.
By the time I get home he's blocked me on Grindr & the cicadas
are so loud I think I might lose it. I eat half a loaf of bread
to soak up the martinis, after which I smoke a Parliament
on the balcony & consider the cicadas. Even scientists
refer to the noise they make as a song, which is the opposite
of what a poet does when they smuggle a scientific fact
into the poem, like how I'm about to tell you it is the male cicadas
you hear & that the noise is produced by a pair of membranous tymbals
contracting on either side of the abdomen & that each species
of cicada produces a unique & specific song that ensures they attract
"only appropriate mates." Being human of course & lacking
any such song, I love a series of inappropriate men. When my friends
are judgmental I tell them *You gotta kiss a few frogs if you*
wanna find your prince—a rationalization for which I can't take credit.
Suffice it to say I'm a millennial so often self-care is indistinguishable
from self-deception. I get hard just thinking about it. I get high
with another one outside the museum. He mispronounces
Gauguin so emphatically that I'm not longer certain
I know how to say it. Even so I go to bed with him.
It isn't even dark yet. And there's some dog shit on the floor
in the corner of his bedroom.

I Can't Relate to the Market-Tested Narratives About Desire

When I'm in a romantic mood I snip
the leafy green stems off strawberries
& smear a white plate with chocolate sauce.
When I've eaten all the strawberries, I lick
my fingers & the plate. I tell myself a joke
& I laugh laugh laugh: it is thrilling
to be this fruitful & wrong, this decadent
& alone. I go to sleep with my phone
& my choice of streaming services.
I wake up & the world is still there—
the aluminosilicate world. The latest
celebrity couple is ill-conceived but
convincingly in love until
the cancelled engagement, the messy
uncoupling. Everyone participates.
The popstar's woe scores the summer
but I can't relate. I might say "traditional."
I might say "the Heterosexuals." I might say
"the romantic comedy is naked" & run
through the theater shouting. On the app
a discreet guy woofs at me. He says he'd love
to see more so I send him
       my literal body.

Melancholy Baby

Once again the dogs in the dog park.
Once again the ever-changing, the elastic
world expands. The long shadows of dusk
grow over. I'm not convinced my body
    is a temple but I can try to be

less sarcastic. Once again the genuine
smile, once again the mustered enthusiasm.
The group text, the group activity. I'm alone
when I want to be otherwise I die
    from embarrassment. Like everyone

I know all the popular songs about love
& I'm just impressed anyone can keep
a straight face. Once again the command
performance. Once again the bathtub, the bomb
    of gardenia & glitter. The water's brief

horizon, my toes, & so on. The poem
writes itself. So what if I spend more money
than I should. When I feel empty, I turn on
the television. A mouth reminds me of your mouth.
    A pair of hands, your hands.

There's Just No Let Up, The Live-Long Night & Day
after Morgan Parker

I'm no good at being a body. I squint
for no reason & assume all the wrong angles.
I'm a supercut of abdominal muscles
& thwarted desires, a skyline of uneasy
expressions. One of these mornings I'm gonna rise up
& dissipate like a hiss of steam for want
of a man's arms around me. Before the movie
somebody's girlfriend is wearing his sweater
while he finds their seats & I just know their life
is perfect. My life too is perfect except
I belong to no one & I keep on feeling more or less
than I should. Lately in lieu of pills I've taken
to keeping cuts of onyx in my pockets
to distract negativity but who knows.
At the end of the unspeakable summer I clear my throat.
The goal is to talk myself into the world.

Judy Garland

I flinched my way through childhood. I couldn't tell you
when I started balking at the sound of my own name
or running in the opposite direction of every pair
of open arms. I just clicked my mother's heels together
three times & rejected the notion that my heart's desire
could possibly be in my own backyard—but there I go again,
transidentifying. For years when asked I said no, then
for a long time nothing, then finally yes, but with
discomfort. Now I'm confrontational as fuck
& automatically resentful of every well-adjusted gay
& every straight guy I've ever blown. Since you ask,
I sleep just fine, but then again, I'm always stoned.
Like a dog my instinct is to bury
anything I consider mine.

Ode to My Sisters' Barbies

In fact, to all of their things! Those dolls
of thermo-molded plastic, yes—perilously proportioned
& teetering! In impossible stilettos! Stitched into
polyvinylidene wigs! Those, yes, but too—their florid
floral wardrobes! Their satin Easter dresses & white
Mary Janes! O exalted hint of heel! O unscuffed
sheen of patent leather! Yes, & too, their zirconia
studs! Their tubes of glittered lip gloss! Their shoebox hoard
of nail polish, kaleidoscope of jars! Yes! & too, their Disney
princesses! Their delicate pajamas! Their fairy-printed
bedsheets! O blessed pink persuasion! O feminine ideal!
Yes! & too, their tears, effusive & allowed!
Their opulent tumble of box braids! Their clatter
of bangled wrists! Their gleaming beads & barrettes!
O effete expressions! O sundry girlhood possessions!
O open world of purple play!

The First Cut is the Deepest

so bless this unpierced moment
this hallowed mirror giving
you back to yourself   resplendent

in mom's work pumps   ball gown
of draped & knotted bedsheet
blue wig of bath towel & hair pins

its cotton cascade   clutching
microphone of lint roller
& sheer fantasy   your little

boy body a sublime corruption
of diva's poses & convincing
lip sync   genderless

as any object in the room—
as the mirror itself
returning now also

your father's reflection
stricken in the doorway
you didn't close behind you

South Bend's Too Quiet at Night

& no one knows why I haven't
run into the hall to scream nonsense

down the stairwell. I was thinking about my body
again: the ultimate incumbrance. These days

I do worry less about money & men I've fucked
only once but it still seems possible

I could live forever in constant pursuit of dick.
I might as well admit that yes, this is about a boy

& years ago. It's about his eyes, their sable
percipience, the timid ambition of his hands

when they touched me. Discerning my secrets,
swearing me to new ones. I couldn't speak

about my body then & he wouldn't speak
at all. Now if I think of him, I think

If he could see me now, but that is hardly ever.
Instead, I say *More* in the heat of some dumb

moment, mouth full of some man's stubble.
More, I demand of the empty sidewalks, mouth full

of rainwater, while all down the block shadows
skirt streetlights like peplum & everything

seems primed for ruin. In every language
there is a word for this, inside each of us

another, hoping to hell.

When I Get Home I Take off My Self

like surprise I've been acting this whole time
now it is late in the evening and there is nothing more
to say except we may never know for sure I hope
that in the future we will get to choose our personalities
from a database of options & upload them
to our brains imagine a personality for any occasion
a new you whenever you want isn't that the logical
conclusion isn't that why people everywhere
are talking like contestants on a reality show looking
directly into every camera saying *I didn't come here*
to make friends I mean it's fine I'm not judging it's just
you can't fathom how vaporous I've become breath
blooming on glass leaving behind nothing right now
my neighbor is banging around in the hallway another
is screaming as always her dog's name last week
the man I miss the most appeared on a bench
at the farmers' market having his lunch beside a wealth
of wild ramps looking just as he's always looked which also
is fine it just further proves my point re: life's outright
indifference its negligence even sometimes its cold shoulder
& what's funny is if he were here now dazzling inscrutable
as ever he would scoff at my self-focused reading
of obviously objective events he would wrinkle his upper lip
& wonder why I am so wed to one way of describing
the contents of a glass but no I had wanted to write
another poem one not presenced by the enormity of
his knuckles or the fulgent mystery of his face alas
he is like the poem a maze you build as you make your way
through it a type of inception I'm here because I have to be
why are you here

Self-Portrait as Tom Ripley in *The Talented Mr. Ripley*
after Alex Dimitrov

When I enter, he is bestride his saxophone
playing de Paul, more shadow than man

before the tall windows & the ceaseless
Neapolitan bay. I begin by collecting

our dross of used glasses, empty bottles
his fiancé's red bikini top, then proffer

my loyalty like tithes, eager disciple
even as he shouts.

How is it that everything feels possible here?

On the train I breathe in
his lapel & do the thing with my neck

that merges our reflections
in the window glass, blurring

our distinctions, twinning us.
Soon, I will be his

wily double, malignant
replicate. For now, all that we say

is to say something else
something more & truer—

Questo é la faccia de Dickie. Questa é la mia faccia.

The war's been over for years
& we have his father's money.

I wear his clothes to know how
he feels beneath them.

American Top 40

Spring is here and the sky
is insignificant. Something to struggle

under. Or it might be an omen, as if to say
there is nothing that is truly worthwhile

except the next poem. A new wig,
a gin martini. Would you improve

by going vegan or giving up red meat
as a friend insists? Or would you

simply go on, avoiding marches
& your neighbors as you have

always done? If the truth hurts
the music, make something up.

At certain times of day
you can achieve optimism.

Anything unpleasant
gets dusted off.

I've Got the World on a String

I walk across my apartment & arrive on a dance floor

I'm all of a sudden dressed for it

I haven't a care

I dance

I fancy myself

I slurp shots that glow in the dark

I set the record for most men kissed in a single night

They give me a crown to wear & a sash

I wonder if I am living in the moment

I am waiting for a man to kill us with a gun

In the morning I wake up next to my boyfriend

He kills the flies in my bedroom & feeds them to the ants in the kitchen

He thinks death can be worthwhile

Says "Namaste, little fly" each time he kills one

He isn't even spiritual, not really

I think it's a little problematic

When I'm sober I tell him "I don't think this is working"

When he's gone I clean everything, even the baseboards

I put out poison for the ants, hang blue strips of fly tape

I wonder if I am living my best life

I throw a party to commemorate the occasion

I invite whomever & they all come

I feel a cultural imperative to be provocative

I say "the tea is piping hot"

I say "the category is: colonizer chic"

I say everything in the gayest voice possible

Lots of upspeak & floating cadences

Lots of sibilance & lilting vowels

I wonder if I am living la vie en rose

At work I scandalize the straight guys by eating a banana

At home I smoke a bowl with Beth via FaceTime

Her boyfriend waits patiently in the background

I am waiting for him to murder her with a gun

I feel contractually obligated to say clever things

I feel like Whoopi Goldberg in the movie "Ghost"

I feel like doing something for the likes

I wonder if I am living on a prayer

I slurp nectar from the mellifluous hours, sweet as I am

I text my ex-boyfriend "u up?"

I text my ex-boyfriend "come over"

Adam Driver

(Beginning with a line from Lynne Tillman)

I'm busy ignoring his long legs.
I just want everything & I want it now.
My problem is I'm a person in the world.
It's June 2021 & there are rainbows
    literally everywhere but I'm skeptical.
Honestly, I think I'd rather be a tree.
I promise it's not an affectation.
All my concerns are contemporary & diffuse.
My interiors all gilded.
& not to get distracted by his long legs on the train
    but there they are.
If I could have any job it would be: popstar.
I'd travel the world, getting married again & again.
Venerated, unspoiled by quotidian disappointments.
Seclusion when the album flops.
But it's June & I wake up hungry as ever.
The breeze bears hot on Broadway
    when I'm leaving work.
There's a function & I am expected.
The problem being I go in my body.
All my friends are in therapy.
My friends all simply cannot.
It's dusk & we've forgotten our manners.
I make a note not to mention his long legs.

Hot Child in the City

Let's go somewhere posh to smoke our cigarettes
& take people's money. One of us can cause a diversion
while the other picks pockets. I have to say, I'm attracted
to the idea. Maybe because I am positively inundated
with options for self-description & attendant
corporations hot to sell them back to me. & all my
money's doing stand-up. & my boss is on my case
again, of course, not to mention my nerves.
But on the phone with Janae I am sufficiently wry
about everything & she laughs at all my jokes.
Looking around I know there's nothing particularly
funny about any of this, actually, unless you're into
that sort of thing: the city's laggard melt, the piles
of dirty laundry, *Mrs. Doubtfire* on HBO. A man's hand
on my jaw but otherwise no identifying features.
& nothing by way of explanation, of course:
you make your own sense or you get used to it, like bad
wallpaper or plumbing in an apartment you can stand
because you know it's only temporary. When the air conditioner
malfunctions I palm my head & declaim against—who? or, what?
God, I guess, given my upbringing, but even if you don't believe
you have to admit that life has a tendency to seem
very intentionally almost sentiently bad a lot of the time
or maybe I'm just making bad choices. I guess
some people do seem content. Naturally, I am suspicious
of anyone who seems to have their shit together
or their student loans. Maybe because I lie awake at night
& imagine my landlord when he's spending my money.

His face is just a big evil smile erupting maniacal laughter.
He's careless with it, my money, though I can see
it brings him great pleasure to spend. Then it is eight AM
& already too hot to go for a walk. I catch the fan's breeze
& look at my phone. I avoid the app that tells me
how much money's in my bank account & the one
that tracks my credit score. Maybe because I feel so automated
sometimes I search myself for a power switch. I know it
must be there somewhere, but I haven't found it.

Practical Advice for Your Queer Son

Don't smoke to escape anything   Instead, cry
for one hour twice a month & have the TV on

constantly   Here, morning takes its sweet-ass time
flowers bloom in all the expected places

& you're anticipating the day your psychic is like
I see nothing beyond next year   because honestly

None of your friends believe
in any sort of afterlife   although it's true

they still geek out over every coincidence
& any instance of déjà-vu   & do try

to be good people   Don't drink to feel
empowered   Instead, raise your glass

& misdirect every outrage   Here, everything
is proof of your goddamn nerves   Don't think

about outside until you can't avoid going there
Sit at your desk & behave nonviolently

& as I said   with the TV on constantly
Grateful for the interruption

of any muse

..

Self Portrait as Forty-Nine Movie Scenes

1

The scene in *Batman Returns* where Michelle Pfeiffer says "Meow" right before the building explodes behind her.

2

The scene in *Batman Returns* where Michelle Pfeiffer crawls on top of Michael Keaton & says, "You're catnip to a girl like me: handsome, dazed, & to die for."

3

The scene in *The Wizard of Oz* where Judy Garland takes her very first steps down the Yellow Brick Road. The camera pans down to her blue socks & the ruby slippers as she begins her fateful journey through the Land of Oz at the very tip of the road's spiral. "Follow the Yellow Brick Road," she says to herself, & the assembled munchkins echo her, & timpani chime with each of her first few steps.

4 - 7

The scenes in *Nocturnal Animals* where Amy Adams is reading Jake Gyllenhaal's manuscript. How I want to read everything like that: breathing audibly, pausing intermittently to take my glasses off & touch my face & wonder.

The scene in *The Color Purple* where Margaret Avery won't let Whoopi Goldberg hide her smile.

The scene in *The Color Purple* where Whoopi Goldberg doesn't cut Danny Glover's throat.

The scene in *Safe* where Julianne Moore is allergic to car exhaust on the freeway.

The scene in *Safe* where Julianne Moore is allergic to the baby shower.

The scene in *Safe* where Julianne Moore is allergic to the dry cleaners.

The scene in *Whatever it Takes* where James Franco is tied to the hotel bed wearing nothing but a leopard print G-string.

The scene in *10 Things I Hate About You* where Julia Stiles reads her poem for Heath Ledger out loud in class in front of everyone & then runs crying out of the room, which fixes everything—Heath Ledger forgives her & kisses her in the parking lot after school.

15

The scene in *Young Adult* where Charlize Theron has a melt down at the baby shower after Patrick Wilson's wife spills sangria on her. "You know, don't bother, it is silk, it's *fucked*," she says when Patrick Wilson's wife tries to dab at her wet blouse. She stands in the street, wine-stained, & says to Patrick Wilson, "I came back for you! For *you!* And I hate this town! It's a hick lake town and it smells of fish shit. But I came back. I just wanted you to know that." & everyone's just watching her, horrified. Her mother and her father and everyone.

16

The scene in *Interview with the Vampire* where Tom Cruise tastes Brad Pitt's neck for the first time. There's so little blood at first that it just looks like they're making out. "Do you still want this? Or have you tasted it enough?" Tom Cruise says. "Enough," says Brad Pitt, & Tom Cruise drops him from their levitation into the muddy Mississippi.

17

The scene in *Interview with the Vampire* where Kirsten Dunst, just realizing she's been made vampire, barges into the room screaming, "WHICH ONE OF YOU DID IT!?!?"

18

The scene in *The Hours* where Meryl Streep has a breakdown in front of Jeff Daniels, how she crumples to the kitchen floor in front of her stainless-steel oven. How she uses the word "presentiment."

The scene in *The Hours* where Nicole Kidman & Stephen Dillane argue at the train station. "I have endured this custody!" Nicole Kidman says, really acting. "I have endured this imprisonment!" I don't care about the fake nose.

20

The scene in *She's All That* where Rachel Leigh Cook gets a make-over from Anna Paquin & she's coming down the stairs into the room where Freddie Prinze, Jr. & her father & a Culkin are waiting for her & "Kiss Me" by Sixpence None the Richer is playing & she really is so pretty but it's very understated.

21

The scene in *Sister Act* where Maggie Smith says, "Girl groups? Boogie-woogie on the piano? What were you thinking?"

22

The scene in *Sister Act* where Whoopi Goldberg stomps her foot three times and says, "Alma, check your battery."

23

The scene in *Sister Act* where Wendy Makkena, the mousy, redhead nun, nails her solo.

24

The scene in *Sister Act II* where Whoopi Goldberg tells Lauryn Hill about Rilke & says, "If you wake up in the morning & you can't think about anything but singing first, then you supposed to be a singer, girl."

25

The scene in *Sister Act II* where they triumph at the All-State Choir Competition even though they were poor & had rappers & hip-hop dancing & performed in their street clothes.

26

The scene in *Now and Then* where Devon Sawa kisses Christina Ricci. "That was the day Roberta stopped taping her breasts," Demi Moore says, in voice over.

27

The scene in *Y Tú Mama Tambien* where Diego Luna & Gael Garcia Bernal kiss each other while they're both getting head from Ana López Morales.

28

The scene in *Y Tú Mama Tambien* where Diego Luna & Gael Garcia Bernal wake up the next morning, naked & beside each other & feeling so gay that Diego Luna has to rush outside to vomit into some shrubs.

29

The scene in *The Talented Mr. Ripley* where Matt Damon & Jude Law are playing chess while Jude Law's taking a bath. Matt Damon teases the water with his fingers & says, clumsily coy, "Hey, I'm cold, can I get in?" & Jude Law's eyes, which have been scrutinizing the chessboard, flash quickly to Matt Damon. For a moment they hold one another's gaze & you aren't certain how Jude Law will respond. But then, "No," he says, after the longest of moments. It's direct, but it taunts like a dare. "I didn't mean with you in it," Matt Damon says, though of course he did mean with him in it. Miles Davis's "Nature Boy" fills every silence. Then Jude Law gets out of the tub & you see his ass while he towels off & if you pause on just the right frame you can see some of his penis & I can't believe this scene happens only thirty minutes into the movie.

30

The scene in *Brokeback Mountain* where Michelle Williams says to Heath Ledger, "You don't go up there to fish!" "Jack Twist?" she says, of Jake Gyllenhaal's character. "Jack *Nasty*." It's the gayest line in the movie.

31

The scene in *Erin Brockovich* where Julia Roberts says to Veanne Cox, "That's all you got lady: two wrong feet in fucking ugly shoes."

32

The scene in *Maleficent* where Angelina Jolie says, "Well, well."

33

The scene in *Fatal Attraction* where Glenn Close says, "I'm not going to be *ignored*, Dan." I know it was popular at the time but her hair in this movie makes me crazy.

34

The scene in *The Silence of the Lambs* where Buffalo Bill asks the senator's daughter, "Say, are you about a size 14?"

35

The scene in *The Bodyguard* where Kevin Costner cuts Whitney Houston's scarf in half to demonstrate the sharpness of his samurai sword.

36

The scene in *The Bodyguard* where Whitney Houston says, "Farmer! You've made me into a raving lunatic!"

37

The scene in *Glitter* where the music video director says of Mariah Carey, "We ask ourselves: is she Black? is she white? We don't know. She's exotic. I want to see more of her breasts."

38

The scene in *Who Framed Roger Rabbit?* where Jessica Rabbit sings "Why Don't You Do Right?"

39

The scene in *The Dark Knight Rises* where Marion Cotillard dies, I don't care.

40

The scene in *Magnolia* where Julianne Moore wears her furs to the pharmacy.

41

The scene in *Wild Things* when Kevin Bacon's taking a shower.

42

The scene in *Thelma & Louise* where Susan Sarandon says, "And in the future? When a woman's crying like that? She isn't having any fun."

43

The scene in *To Wong Foo, Thanks for Everything! Julie Newmar* where Patrick Swayze says, "When a lady says no, she means: get your hand off my dick, buddy!"

44

The scene in *To Wong Foo, Thanks for Everything! Julie Newmar* where they use gay magic to make suitable the dusty motel room.

45

The scene in *To Wong Foo, Thanks for Everything! Julie Newmar* where Wesley Snipes says, "It's an affront to the very delicacy of my nature."

46

The scene in *Dirty Dancing* where Jerry Orbach says to Jennifer Gray, "You looked wonderful out there."

47

The scene in *Dirty Dancing* where Jane Brucker sings "Hula Hana."

48

The scene in *The First Wives Club* where they're all fighting
& Goldie Hawn says, "I *do* have feelings! I'm an actress—I
have *all* of them!"

49

The scene at the party in *All About Eve* where Bette Davis
insults all of her friends & says, "Am I being rude?" &
George Saunders tells her, "You're maudlin and full of self-
pity—you're magnificent."

You're maudlin and full of self-pity—you're magnificent!

· · ·

So Far the New Year's No Different From the Old

Thaw, still, in the planet's coldest regions. Fires ringing
entire continents. Lunatics on every screen, frothing white
promises and dog whistles. I was very stoned when I explained
to Beth about the End Times. I told her: earthquakes and famines.
Confusion of seasons. Nations in anguish. War everywhere
& rumors of it. It was the weather got us talking, the freaky weather:
too warm for January, Australia up in flames. It doesn't mean anything
that there are Christians who believe that climate change is a sign
of Christ's second coming. "The Media" call them *climate change
deniers* but this isn't really accurate as it suggests that they deny
the existence of climate change when in fact what they deny is
humanity's active role in exacerbating the crisis. & that there's anything
we can do to curb its effects. Doesn't matter. Proof, only, that one's Truth
is usually contingent upon one's personal interpretation of The Data.
I can understand the sentiment when people say *Can't we all just get along*
but I would rather write this on my eyeballs than hear That Man
garble through another live press conference. He'll likely destroy democracy;
he can't have television too. O Television! When I was a kid people talked
all the time about the ozone layer & its many holes, but I haven't heard anyone
mention it in I swear to God twenty years. I still don't know exactly what it is.
I could never really visualize it. I guess maybe it's gone now, completely.

One of the scariest movies ever is *Fern Gully*: its villain: the pollutant-loving

Hexxus, a fluid, black, quasi-humanoid smoke figure burlesquing

through the rainforest, oddly sexual, singing: *filthy brown acid rain /*

pouring down like egg chow mein. Voiced by Tim Curry. Siphoning life

out of everything & loving it. Horrible. Just horrible. I had my mother

stitch a SAVE THE RAINFOREST patch to my bookbag. I saved

my allowance for a month & donated it to the Rainforest Foundation Fund.

It was no place I desired to go but I did think it should be there.

If you google "is the planet dying" you will generate millions of results

none of them comforting. I'm mad because I want all the trappings of modernity

but none of the hassle. & recycling is so complicated they sent us instructions

in the mail. Illustrated instructions. One of the saddest movies ever is

The Land Before Time: in the wake of environmental disaster, a group

of orphaned dinosaurs set off on a journey to find the Great Valley, a fabled,

fecund paradise amidst global famine. Traumatic, for a child: the murderous

Sharptooth, blood-mad & flesh-hungry. Littlefoot's dying mother, her limp

long neck. Essex Hemphill, also dead, predicting my life: *I have a cat*

and a thousand poems. This morning it occurred to me that if I were to die

tomorrow I would leave behind basically nothing at all of value & Shane

would have to find someone to cover my shifts at the bookstore.

January 2020

51 Reasons to Give Up Hope

1. The eroding lakeshore, the homes dangling from the dunes' new cliffs
2. The corn on my right pinky toe
3. The likelihood of my advancing too far professionally
4. The white Lyft driver who asked if I was mixed
5. Because "You *sound* white but I can tell you're *not* white"
6. Excusing her curiosity with the fact of her biracial children
7. The handful of Jolly Ranchers I gave her, I don't know why
8. The Oscarlessness of Alfre Woodard
9. Sean, who mysteriously stopped texting
10. My carbon footprint
11. The word "discharge"
12. A weeks' worth of dishes moldering in the sink
13. My student loans
14. My nephew, born three months early
15. Craving opioids
16. Respiring meconium
17. My mother, tasked with caring for him
18. Insurance premiums
19. Cable news
20. My Aunt Lori, who died last summer
21. Suddenly
22. My grandfather, also dead
23. Jeremy, living with some girl in Rockford
24. My brother
25. My brother
26. His girl
27. The list of substances delivered with the baby

28. The arctic harp seals, birthing their young on melting ice floes
29. And I might never quit smoking
30. The Electoral College
31. Twitter
32. Our carceral system
33. Karlie Kloss
34. Jack, who kissed me just once, outside of McCormick's, before I never saw him again
35. My succulents, refusing to thrive
36. The word "curdle"
37. Election season
38. Oscar season
39. The water in Flint
40. The tendonitis in my left knee
41. Minimum wage
42. "A living wage"
43. The stranger who overdosed outside my apartment the night before Thanksgiving
44. Athleisure
45. Employment-based healthcare
46. How long it's been since I last saw a dentist
47. And I can never correctly pronounce the word "eschewed"
48. And people come & go so quickly here
49. And this pen is running out of ink
50. And the state of my toenails
51. And the price of a pack of cigarettes rivals what I make in an hour

I Honestly Don't Think I Can Stand It

I am so deeply
regretful. Will I die
trying to decipher
the secret meaning
of everything? New
housing developments,
your jawline. I recognize
life for the lonely
hurl toward nothing
that it is but this
doesn't make me
any freer. I spend
so much of my time
making money
for other people.
I understand so little
about my pay stub.
The news. The United
States. Its Constitution.
"Dearest, I feel certain
I am going mad again."
Dearest, our bodies
are useless, utterly.
Like this, we carry on—
all our clumsy patterns,
our gauche affairs, all
thoroughly inelegant.
When it is still too cold

a mourning dove alights
on my balcony railing—
down-breasted, nonplussed,
one marble eye returning
a shard of taupe sky
to the taupe sky.

The Heart of the Matter

If I had any money I would leave the country. There aren't any people here and I know them all. I only want to express myself but you can't say things like "nobody loves me" or "my life is completely empty" and expect to be taken seriously. In life or in poetry. Unfortunately what we have at the heart of the matter is a bloody beating heart situated at too great a distance from a perfectly rational brain to fall under its influence. When he leaves he leaves a negative space but as someone who thinks critically I know it is in the gaps we find true meaning. Still, what I would like most is to be inside all of it, with no awareness, least of all of myself. Why can't a whale symbolize a whale? Why must a green light portend deeper meaning? My great heroic flaw is that I ask too many questions. Or that I bite my nails. I don't have any faith yet still I hope this cigarette lasts forever. I hope someone famous shows up right this second. I hope I die with your huge cock in my ass only you don't immediately realize it & you haven't come yet so you keep going.

Some Personal News

I'm drinking more water.
So far this year, I'm averaging more
steps-per-day than last year, but my headphones
are louder. You'd be so proud
of the many changes I've been making.
For instance, these days, I'm almost never seen
at parties in my bear suit, grizzlying
the perimeter, cocktail balanced
in my claws, growling for honey or whatever
bears want. & I've almost completely stopped hissing
at strangers who are walking too slowly
when I'm trying to get somewhere.
& I never smoke in public these days—
almost never. Eventually the retrograde
will end & we'll have nothing on which to hang
our failures. Everyone is very anxious about this
& other calamities, pending or otherwise.
I'm taking care of myself "for the revolution"
which they say is definitely coming.

It Could Happen to You

The city is discouraging enough without the heatwaves
& parking tickets. Will you ever make it. Will you ever
find work. What are the chances someone here

has a gun. What are your roommates saying when
you aren't home. Do you care. Are you taking more
than your share from the community garden. Has anyone

noticed. Are your brothers safe. Will you die in a mass
shooting. Does your shrink talk about you in the hypothetical
to her friends. Would it bother you. Are you fooling

anyone. Suppressing the prickly suspicion that dreams
are not of this time you go after them. Grind. Exfoliate.
Pumice flaws from your skin until you are flawless.

At least visibly. Floss, non-colloquially. Pay the parking
tickets. Collect vinyl, like everyone is. Clean your toilet.
Change your sheets. Console a friend

whose dog has just died. Publish, but you are not fulfilled.
Then, in a park, pigeons scattered by children ruin a picture
you're trying to take of the sunset for a poet you follow on Twitter

who is just as lonely as you are lonely. You're mad at first,
but after all, it is only a picture, just a sunset, & the children
don't know what they've done, nor the spooked pigeons.

Wedding Bell Blues

It's been spring for forty-five days & I am not at all in love.
I might forgive my neighbors their lusty peonies, the mint
teeming across the grass, but not the libertine daffodils
which gape erogenously: I too have depths
for plumbing. If I remember J's thumb
parting my lips, I'll send him flirty texts, for
it's the pleasure he took in me that I miss, the relish
of his discovering. All across the city people are tripping
from Ubers to embraces to bars & I am spitting this
into the wind misting fishily off the lake. The shoreline
erodes at a measurable pace & a group of bridesmaids
struggles across the beach toward the season's first wedding.
I'll be honest, I haven't even tried to parse meaning
from their graceless stumbling over the sand, the murmur
of their gowns frenzied on the breeze.

Torch Song

Autumn stalks the distance, a wolf
at the forest's edge, biding its time.
Nothing astonishes but the trees,
glad to relinquish their green. . .

How quickly my body has recovered
its indifference! Here, which you have traded
for the neon novelty of elsewhere. . .I prefer
your interference, your chinos

folded neatly on my chair. . .But I have written
that poem already, where your going is described
as an endless vein unspooling from my arm. . .
I would rather unhinge our geography, pluck miles

from the map like lint pills, but where were we
when I found you, bearded & laughing
in bisexual light?

Maine

There are so many ways to feel
like a fool. My Soundcloud, for instance.
The chapbook I self-published last year
at considerable personal expense
but never distributed. My horoscope
telling me, "Give love if you want to
receive it, Gemini," but failing to specify
to whom, exactly. So you see. I'm staying
at a hotel where the swimming pool
is so full of dead leaves you can't see
the water but people are using it anyway.
Come get me.

Nocturne in My Favorite Coat

Meanwhile, the moon's bone white
& waxing crescent—my God, it's winking
isn't it? I do that too
on less moderate nights than this
& when my legs are bare
against the encroaching
dimmet. I'm just
cleaned up for work
in the meantime.
You laugh but you know
I mean it. I laugh because
I'm hardly joking:
in all my daydreams I am that lawless
& gaudy, arriving everywhere feeling armed
& rich. Winking too. Just like the moon
I phase. Am full. Am winking.
Am thumbnail, naturally.
& so modern.
When I put my legs up
& dissociate there's nothing
like it. The moon wishes.
I put on lipstick when I want
to smoke a cigarette. Wink
if I want to. Really living.
When the bills come due I'll get ornery
& radical. It's not enough
that I log on every day
& consume consume consume.

It's embarrassing.
How much I like buying things.
But who doesn't want.
It's midnight & I need
more cigarettes so I wear my long coat
to the bodega. It's my favorite. I flirt
with the guy behind the counter
who's too underpaid to notice.
He hasn't got time for my nonsense.
I get it. On the street no one but the moon
can tell I'm just going home to smoke
& put my legs up. At least I hope I look mysterious—
walking so fast & with such purpose
my coat billowing.

And Still the Lights Have Not Gone Out

I'm sorry, but these geraniums look like rainstorms. These people all talk like dumb babies. If you are so good, why are these rabbits wearing scrubs, and where are they taking me? I love it when a morning pops like Sprite but I hate seeing clearly, *This is you, living.* These cookies taste like mushroom clouds. This straitjacket says Chanel. My head is about to fall off but never mind, I'm gonna keep on dancing. Because I must! Because these shoes make me feel anointed! Because the whole world is lampooning me with carnations! Because this is the ghastly sputtering halt of the earth & we are glamorous! & the sun! The sun is fuchsia! & the Earth is dying. Outside, everyone we know is gathering on the polyester lawn. They are fierce & flagitious & posing for pictures while several girls hiding behind a cardboard shrub are shitting themselves uncontrollably. Someone somewhere likes it. & there are Chihuahuas everywhere. Real chihuahuas. People are crushing them beneath their feet, but it is unavoidable, there are so many, you mustn't blame them.

Abeyance

Who knows what else we did.
Cleared inboxes, hung new curtains.
I in my smoke-blue apartment washed
my face & contemplated empire. Still life
with bad news & hair dye. Self portrait
with mugwort & thistle. It was hard
to make any progress. I ran the tap & wept
for my people. History rolled up
with a blunt, sneered in the doorway.
Sanctimonious as an ex. Calling me
yellow. I was shrugged shoulders & cigarette ash
flicked at the fireplace. (No fire.) Limpid
nonchalance. You weren't supposed to pay
attention. That was one of the rules.

In the Street the Young Men Are Marching

in unison & varying stages of undress.
They are all unarmed & semi-hard & stomping
wedding cakes & birth certificates.
They are singing & vomiting glitter
& turning perfect pirouettes. I tell you
My body is a mausoleum. You say
Some of my best friends are surgeons
& commence to cut me open
& pluck out these dead things. . .

It Might as Well Be Spring

I am mostly bewildered
by most of what you tell me.
I wouldn't even believe you
except your face is so damn
believable. Your fucking face.
I hug you around your neck
& *say kid you oughta be*
in pictures but I don't quite
nail the mid-Atlantic accent
& you don't entirely get it,
not entirely. You're too well-
adjusted, probably, for pastiche
& shouldn't be addressed
so casually. But isn't it
romantic! & aren't we a pair!
Me, a veritable playlist
for regression! You with
your phone that plays
any song you tell it to!
Something melancholy
I say, but not too sad.
You're good at it. I'm good
at a few things but nothing
so practical. You like me
this way, or so you tell me.
& really, have I any choice
but to believe you? You're here
after all, scrambling eggs

for me, making a mess
of my kitchen, & your phone
is connected to my Bluetooth
speaker. Somewhere else
a crocodile is weeping
over their own breakfast
for the simple fact that
(if you can believe it)
this is what crocodiles do—
properly ashamed,
maybe, by their glut,
or maybe conflicted over
the means of its acquisition.
But here—*here*—in my apartment
post-coital (& the funk of it!!
& the smell of you on my breath!!!)
with these fluffy yellow eggs
& this sturdy multi-grain toast
& the fancy preserves
from the grocer on Wabansia
I never go in but you insisted—
& the abhorrently expensive juice
we bought there also—
& likewise the bag of everything
bagels, the unpronounceably
branded cream cheese—
here, amongst our own spoils
if I happen to lean back
in my chair with my knees
pressed against the table edge
to observe you through
the scrim of steam rising

from my coffee as you
munch toast & ignore
a call from your brother—
if you happen to look up
& catch me looking & you say
"What?" I will say "Nothing."
& should you look away
for a moment & a moment later
look back & discover me still looking
& again you ask "What?" again
I will say "Nothing, nothing."
& if we go through it again my love
& even one more time
forgive me
forgive me
I only know how this is done
in the movies.

. . . .

Ideal-I

Is good with money. Pays bills on time, every time. Never overdraws bank account. Has only the tiniest amount of credit card debt. And has good credit. Is aggressively paying off student loans. Doesn't smoke cigarettes. Doesn't buy cat food at 7-11. Doesn't buy anything at 7-11. Eats better. Drinks more water. Isn't high all the time. Isn't on Facebook. Has read Proust. Doesn't show up without invitation. Didn't make a scene. Isn't so passive-aggressive. Is happy for you. Sincerely. Is less anxious. Doesn't flirt with straight men. Didn't wear that sweater, you know the one. Doesn't still check your Tumblr from time to time. Doesn't tweet nefariously or @ celebrities. Doesn't think of at least three mean things to say to someone immediately upon meeting them. Can do math. Owns, doesn't rent. Is current on car payment. Regrets fewer sexual partners. Hasn't smoked two bowls already today. Didn't write this stoned. Takes a commonly acceptable number of showers per week. Calls father more often. Is an adequately informed member of the electorate. Doesn't stream movies illegally. Doesn't read the comments. Starts each day with a well-rounded breakfast. Is closer to brothers. Didn't sing "Bad Romance" at karaoke that one time. Has an opinion about *Citizen Kane*. Isn't listening to *Blue* by Joni Mitchell right now. On vinyl. Doesn't argue with strangers online. Posts fewer selfies. Visits grandmother more often. Didn't do that to you. Is never scared. Isn't worried about the future but does have a 401(k). Doesn't think too much about dying but does have life insurance. Didn't get carried away. Doesn't, as a rule. Doesn't look back in anger. Doesn't look back.

I've Got a Lot of Living to Do

Good morning, Bob!

Good morning, America!

Good morning, drool-damp pillow!

Good morning, French Press!

Good morning, first Parliament Light!

Good morning, first defecation!

Good morning, Mr. Roker!

Good morning, Shark Bite, dregs of last night's bowl!

Good morning, neighbor's Rottweiler, taking a shit out back!

Good morning, neighbor, watching your Rottweiler take a shit!

Good morning, rangy maple, your trunk's mossy couture!

Good morning, iPhone!

Good morning, Twitter!

Good morning, 354 followers!

Good morning, supine day!

Good morning, October, crisp as an apple!

Good morning, algid blue sky, white cloud crowns!

Good morning, Serious Joggers™ in your Serious Jogging Outfits™!

Good morning, preschoolers, leashed chain gang of toddlers exiting the park!

Good morning, Leigh at my Starbucks who never remembers my order!

Good morning, woman on the sidewalk outside of Walgreen's, balancing yourself against a bike dock, stuffing gauze into the backs of your shoes!

Good morning, guy in sweatpants, walking your dog! Good morning visible
outline of your penis!

Good morning, gray squirrel, vertical on that tree!

Good morning, smaller image of this as captured by my iPhone!

Good morning, Instagram!

Good morning, Mayfair! Good morning, Brannan!

Good morning, fattened rat, scurrying from your night of pillaging smorgasbords!

Good morning, Blue Line!

Good morning, woman wearing silk scrunchie!

Good morning, grimy escalator!

Good morning, skyscrapers!

Good morning, proto-police state!

Good morning, late capitalism!

Good morning, anachronous water puddle!

Good morning, cowering tourists!

Good morning, harried & hurrying business folk!

Good morning, wheezing city buses!

Good morning, teens drumming on buckets!

Good morning, injured or mutated pigeon!

Good morning, abundant city!

Good morning!
Good morning!

Good morning!

Notes & Acknowledgements

The poem "Self Portrait as Tom Ripley in *The Talented Mr. Ripley*"
is inspired by and owes a great formal debt to Alex Dimitrov's
poem "Self Portrait as Daisy Buchanan in *The Great Gatsby*," from
his collection *Together & By Ourselves*. This poem also incorporates
lines from the screenplay for *The Talented Mr. Ripley*, written by
Anthony Minghella, from Patricia Highsmith's novel.

The Essex Hemphill quote in "So Far the New Year's No Different
from the Old" comes from his poem, "Fixin' Things."

"I Honestly Don't Think I Can Stand It" incorporates a sentence
from a letter written by Virginia Woolf to her husband, Leonard.

"There's Just Not Let Up, the Live-Long Night & Day" is partially
inspired by a poem by Morgan Parker.

"Adam Driver" begins with a line from Lynne Tillman's novel
American Genius: A Comedy.

. . .

My deepest gratitude to the journals, editors, and readers where
some of these poems initially appeared, sometimes in dramatically
different incarnations:

"Wedding Bell Blues" in *The Chicago Reader*
"Who Could Ask for Anything More?" "Melancholy Baby" "There's
  Just No Let Up" and "Judy Garland" (as "Sonnet") in *Columbia*

Poetry Review
"Hot Child in the City" in *Court Green*
"The Heart of the Matter" in *Hobart*
"Nocturne in My Favorite Coat," "It Could Happen to You," and
  "Abeyance" in *Landfill*
"Maine" in *Queen Mob's Teahouse*
"Adam Driver," "It Might as Well Be Spring," and "Some Personal
  News" in the *Oyez Review.*

. . .

I am eternally grateful to the people who appear in these poems,
either by name, essence, or effigy. My particular thanks and love
to: my mother, who is my life's first great and enduring love; Nick
Rossi, whose emotional, intellectual, and creative support have
been invaluable, and whose friendship has been one of the great
surprises and joys of my life; Kate Wilson, who has taught me
so much about care—what it is, what it looks, how to do it; the
writers and educators whose example, insight, and instruction
were instrumental as I crafted many of these poems, and whose
fingerprints are on every page of this book; Lambda Literary
and the 2021 retreat fellows, for their bravery, generosity, and
community; and finally, my family, whose love and support
nourishes and challenges me everyday.

Chad Morgan is a writer and educator. He lives in Chicago.